BOOK SOLD
NO LONGER R.H.P.L.
PROPERTY

RICHMOND HILL
PUBLIC LIBRARY

JUN 13 2006

CENTRAL LIBRARY
905-884-9288

An Evil Twin Publications Book

**PHOTOGRAPHS BY NICHOLAS ZINNER**

ST. MARTIN'S GRIFFIN
NEW YORK

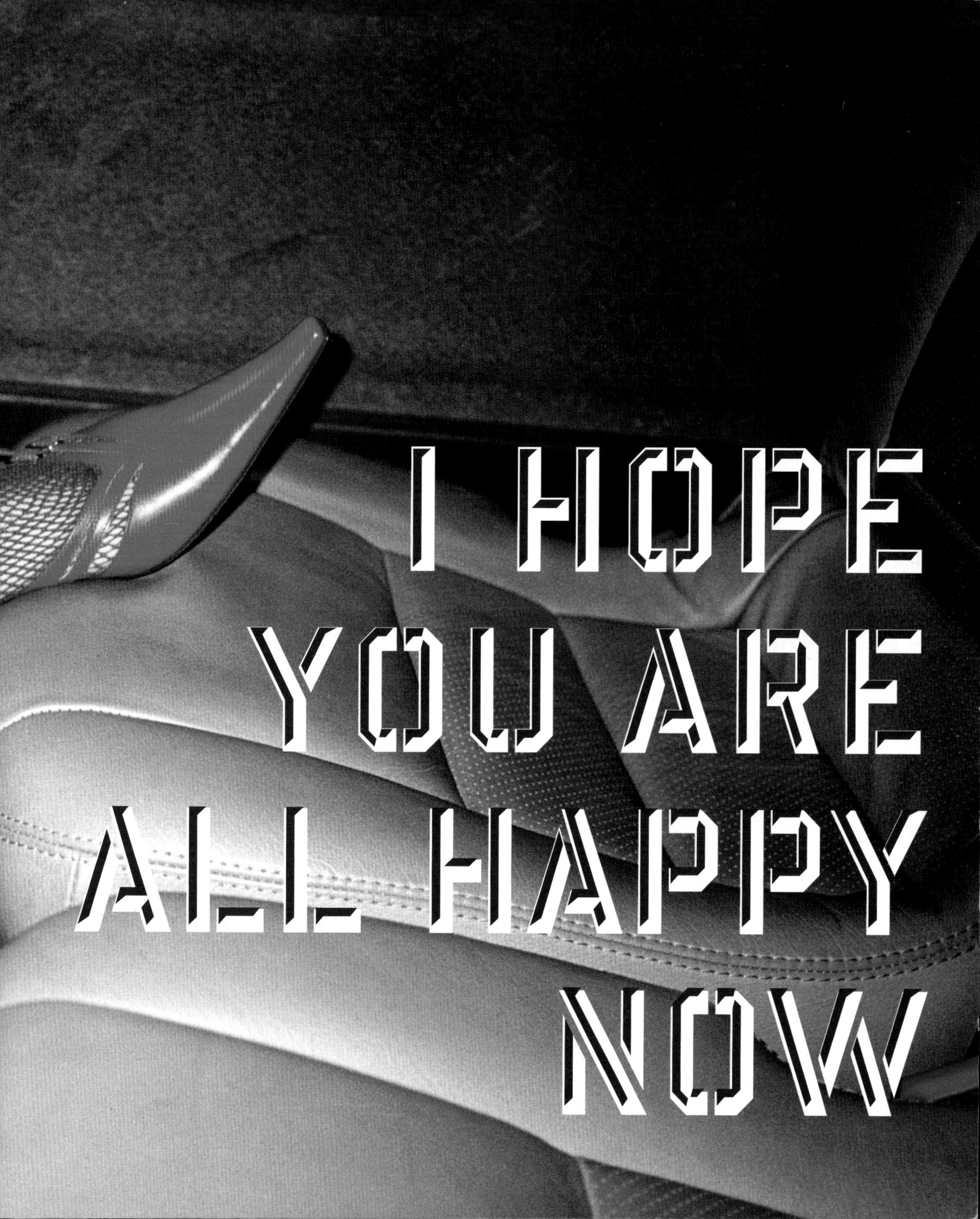
I HOPE
YOU ARE
ALL HAPPY
NOW

# I HOPE YOU ARE ALL HAPPY NOW

Copyright © 2005 by Nicholas Zinner.

All photographs copyright © 2005 by Nicholas Zinner.

All rights reserved. Printed in Thailand.
No part of this book may be used or reproduced
in any manner whatsoever without written permission
except in the case of brief quotations embodied in critical
articles or reviews.

For information, address
St. Martin's Press
175 Fifth Avenue
New York, NY 10010

www.stmartins.com


Book design by Stacy Wakefield at Evil Twin Publications.

Evil Twin Publications
P.O. Box 1318
Cooper Station
New York, NY 10276

www.EvilTwinPublications.com

"Never Mind the Formula" © 2005 by Jim Jarmusch.
"Nick Zinner Is a Fan" © 2005 by Zachary Lipez.
"The Unobstructed View" © 2005 by David Cross.
Interview with Nicholas Zinner by Jesse Pearson © 2005 by Nicholas Zinner.

Title page photographs by Nicholas Zinner:
Koala, Sydney, October 2003
Red Shoes, London, June 2003

Library of Congress Cataloging-in-Publication Data Available Upon Request

ISBN 0-312-34091-5
EAN 978-0312-34091-9

First Edition: September 2005
10 9 8 7 6 5 4 3 2 1

Thank you to: Asif Ahmed, Ilirjana Alushaj, Ben Blackwell, Guy Blakesly, Carrie Brownstein, Dave Burton, Brian Chase, Christina Cho, Cody Critcheloe, David Cross, Patrick Daughters, Aaron Diskin, Jenny Eliscu, Larry Fink, Nicholas Forte, James Fuentes, Amber Gayle, Laurent Girard and Lexington Labs, Julian Gross, Har Mar Superstar, Nako Hashizume, Rebecca Heller and St. Martin's Press, Heidi Hofmann, Jim Jarmusch, Jon Spencer Blues Explosion, Spike Jonze, Christian Joy, Nadia Korinth, The Liars, Zachary Lipez, The Locust, Marilyn Manson, Jack Martin, The Melvins, Eddy Moretti, Aliya Naumoff, Conor Oberst, Karen Orzolek, Arthur Owens, Monica Pa, Jesse Pearson, Lee Ranaldo and Sonic Youth, Solana Rivas, Mick Rock, Stephen Shore, Sam Speigel, Mark Spitz, TV On The Radio, Brooke Vermillion, Jack White, Meredith, Janet & Stephen Zinner, and all the kids in the crowd.

RICHMOND HILL
PUBLIC LIBRARY

JUN 13 2006

CENTRAL LIBRARY
905-884-9288

# NEVER MIND THE FORMULA

*Brian, Patrick, and Nick in an Elevator, London 2003*

With his camera, Nick Zinner has been noting observations of an unusual life. This book assembles his offhand photographs by allowing them to refer to one another in the same way Zinner's camera refers to the world he's moving through. It's a twenty-first century rock 'n' roll world, but the cumulative affect isn't only that. These are images of circumstance, each page becoming its own configuration.

For at least the past decade I've been drawn to a trend in photography that first emerged in a Japanese magazine called *Out of Photographers*. Its pages were filled only with snapshots taken by Japanese teenagers — mundane, silly, sad, stupid, beautiful artifacts of daily teenage life. (The true godfather of all this is most likely the Japanese photographer Nobuyoshi Araki, one of my very favorites, whose pseudo-amateur black-and-white images of personal hardcore sex interspersed with photos of deserted Tokyo back streets, fluorescent vending machines, details of hotel-room floors with tossed-off clothing, telephone cords, and ashtrays have elevated photography to an ethereal new dimension.)

I've been happy to find Nick's photos following an adjacent trajectory, and blurring similar lines in the process. On one hand, this book can be looked at as cultural anthropology (clothes, hairstyles, tattoos, attitude, food, decor, incidental furniture, architecture, and infrastructure). For me, though, it's more of a photo diary, really — but one that chooses not to make any distinction between what's dramatic and what's mundane.

Sometimes Zinner seems drawn to colors and shapes, or just haphazard compositions. At other times he finds in those within view human fragility, or maybe fatigue, or ecstasy, or boredom.

His photos of fans taken from the stage are striking in their near-abstract mix of artificial light and human bodies. Often faces are distinct, each one a kind of micro-portrait of the spirit of rock 'n' roll (or expression in general). From the stage, the lens of Zinner's camera becomes a mirror, and this time he blurs the line between subject and object, between fan and performer, between perceiver and perceived.

Then there are the personal artifacts, the details — airplanes and sky, hotel rooms and toilets, torn stockings, bruises, buses, side streets, televisions . . . And the cool thing is he does all of this without any intention of the "photo as metaphor" or "image as aphorism" kind of shit.  These images truly feel unconsciously offhand.

One last thing about this book: although it also deftly sidesteps the cliches of the "rock 'n' roll lifestyle" bullshit, there *is* a very strong, almost tangible energy inside these images — a sincere "lust for life" (respect to Iggy). And finding energy in stillness, and poetry in the smaller details of daily life (minus the cliches), is a rare and beautiful quality. Never mind the formula — here's *I Hope You Are All Happy Now*.

— Jim Jarmusch
New York, January 2005

14

15

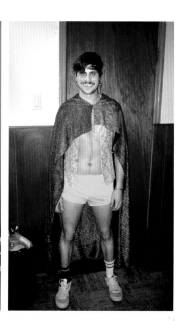

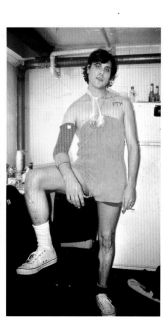

25

# NICK ZINNER IS A FAN

I try to guess where each crowd shot is taken. Through my own biases and parochial filter, I check out the kids' skin and outfits. The Midwest is slightly — ahem — cherubic. The West Coast kids love their accessories. In the New York photos (I can tell it's New York by the ex-friends in the back row), the kids are, of course, perfect — even if by most accounts they don't dance around much. Sweden and San Francisco are easy — there is some sort of Chunnel between them where all the sullen black-haired girls of the world commute back and forth, solely to attend shows. In the Berlin shots, the crowd is more critical, the hair asymmetrical. The Chicagos, Canadas, Sydneys of the world, I have to admit, confound me.

I fear crowds. Not to the point of phobia but well past dislike. I don't attend protests and the last stadium show I went to was AC/DC, because it was AC/DC. I don't like being touched when I'm sober, and I don't like strangers groping and sweating around me. That's what other people's apartments are for.

I used to take comfort in the belief that Nick Zinner was in my camp on this. I first encountered him in the mid-'90s at Williamsburg's Sweetwater Tavern. (It's called something else now — but who cares, we don't go there anymore.) On any given

PRECEDING PAGE: CONEY ISLAND JULY 2002

Tuesday, Sweetwater overflowed with the neighborhood's new punks, new squatters, new design interns, and ex-members of Reagan Youth and the Swans. Nick could be found lurking in the corner with his hyper-coiffed then-bandmates, studiously avoiding eye contact with EVERYONE. Nick didn't talk to the girls, Nick didn't talk to me. Nick, like so many of us, preferred to remain a voyeur. The notion of him someday standing before thousands of screaming delinquents and taking bizarrely empathetic photos of them would have then been dismissed as highly unlikely.

I don't know when Nick departed from my worldview and acquired his ability to see more in crowds than I could. (I've never asked. We have a comfortable subject range, and we stick to it.) But at some point, what I assume started out as purely a documenting device became a reverse fan letter. Don DeLillo, whom I've probably never read, says the future belongs to crowds. I've always found this notion terrifying. Nick's view of crowds is warmer, more embracing, and, in the end, more convincing. In his photos girls flirt, kids give the finger, and the dude in the Naked Raygun shirt sulks. In these crowds the majority (maybe because we know they're actually a minority) becomes less threatening than adorable. No fascistic rage, no messy inner lives, no homogenized teenyboppers. Just really bad kids with white belts and sinister intentions, threatening to engulf the dopey overgrown adolescents onstage. And Nick takes his photo like, "Oh, that's OK. I'm glad you're here. I like you, too."

— Zachary Lipez
New York, January 2005

MELBOURNE OCTOBER 2003

NOTTINGHAM FEBRUARY 2003

TOKYO OCTOBER 2003

39

SAN DIEGO  OCTOBER 2002
NEW YORK CITY  FEBRUARY 2002
BRUSSELS  APRIL 2004

DETROIT  MAY 2003
NEW YORK CITY  OCTOBER 2002
SHEFFIELD  APRIL 2002

NEW YORK CITY  APRIL 2003            LOS ANGELES  MARCH 2004
CLEVELAND  MAY 2003             HOUSTON  NOVEMBER 2003
CHICAGO  APRIL 2003             SAN DIEGO  APRIL 2003

TORONTO AUGUST 2003

42

HAMBURG AUGUST 2003

43

BRISTOL MARCH 2003 / FLORENCE APRIL 2004
SAN FRANCISCO SEPTEMBER 2003 / SYDNEY DECEMBER 2002

44

BIRMINGHAM APRIL 2004 / LONDON JUNE 2003
DETROIT NOVEMBER 2003 / SHEFFIELD FEBRUARY 2003

LONDON  APRIL 2002
MELBOURNE  OCTOBER 2003

PHILADELPHIA  APRIL 2003
OKLAHOMA CITY  MARCH 2004

MANCHESTER APRIL 2004

TUCSON MARCH 2004

50

OSAKA OCTOBER 2003

51

KANSAS CITY MARCH 2002

MELBOURNE DECEMBER 2003

CHICAGO NOVEMBER 2003

HOUSTON NOVEMBER 2003

57

LONDON JUNE 2002

LONDON APRIL 2002

59

TOKYO OCTOBER 2003

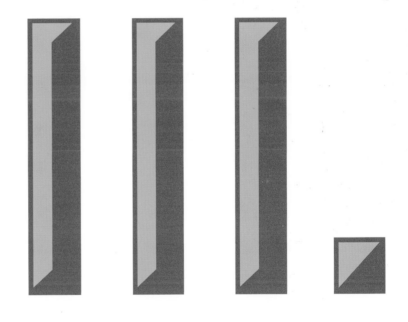

BUS BREAKDOWN, CALIFORNIA, OCTOBER 2002. ON TOUR WITH THE LIARS. WE MANAGED TO COAST INTO SAN DIEGO SAFELY WITH NO BRAKES AND A BUSTED STARTER. THE ROAD, NORTH DAKOTA, APRIL 2003. THIS COULD POSSIBLY ALSO BE IN MONTANA. RUE ZINNER, BRUSSELS, APRIL 2004. A TINY STREET NAMED AFTER A HISTORIC BELGIAN GARDENER. KAREN, TEXAS, MARCH 2002. STRETCHING AFTER AN EIGHT-HOUR MINIVAN RIDE ON YYY'S FIRST TOUR.

HIGHWAY SKY, MISSOURI, MARCH 2002. GAS, FOOD, AND LODGING; AD NAUSEAM . . . GUN SHOP, LINCOLN, AUGUST 2004. DOWN THE STREET FROM THE STUDIO WHERE THE BRIGHT EYES LP I PLAYED ON WAS RECORDED. SOUNDCHECK, PHILADELPHIA, JULY 2004. FOR THOSE ABOUT TO ROCK, WE SALUTE YOU. SOUTHGATE HOUSE, KENTUCKY, OCTOBER 2002. A GHOST WILL HOWL THROUGH THE STAGE MONITORS HERE SHOULD SHE NOT APPROVE OF YOUR BAND.

HALLWAY IN THE HOTEL CONGRESS, TUCSON, OCTOBER 2002. JOHN DILLINGER WAS CAPTURED SHORTLY AFTER FLEEING A FIRE HERE IN 1934. IT IS ALSO HAUNTED.

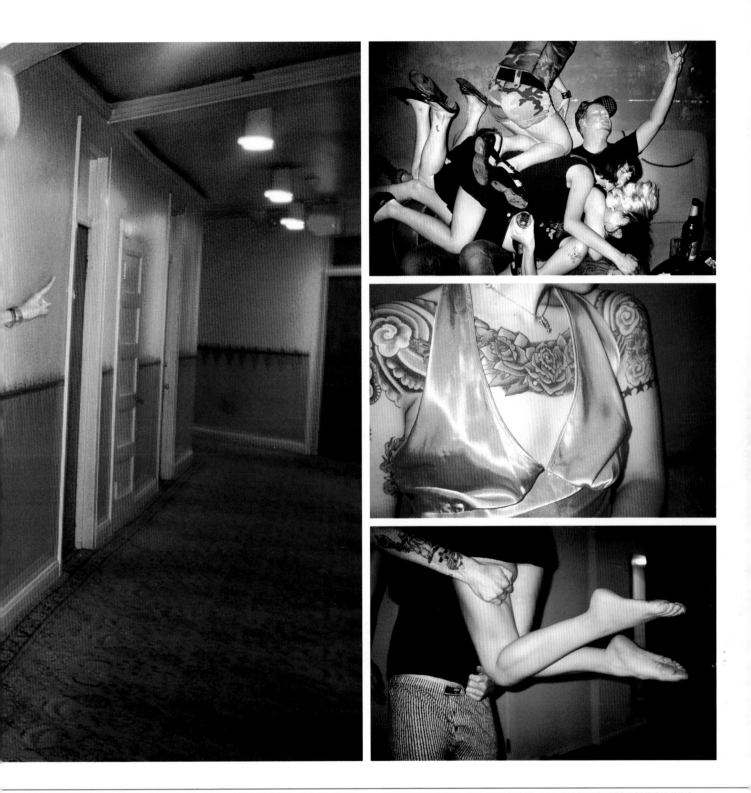

ABSINTHE BAR, BERLIN, APRIL 2003.　JESSICA'S TATTOOS, NYC, SEPTEMBER 2003.　MEGAN'S LEGS, LONDON, JUNE 2003.

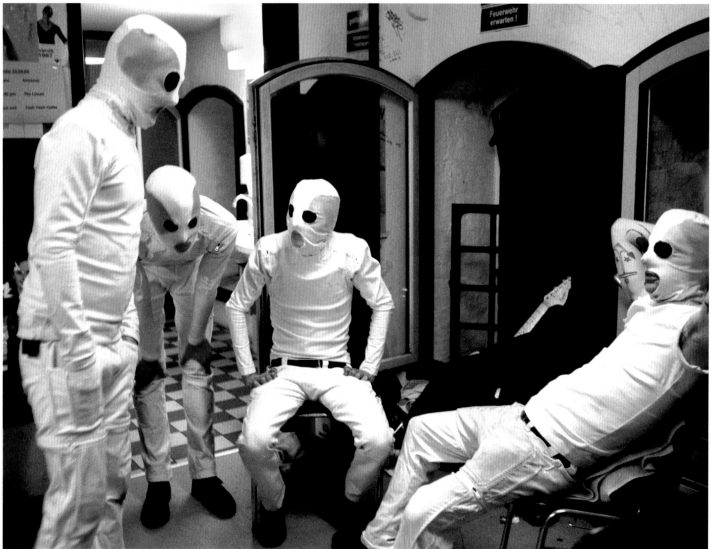

THE QUEEN MOTHER IS DEAD, LONDON, MARCH 2002. FERRY, UK, MARCH 2002. FROM UK TO FRANCE. KAREN ON TRAIN, IRELAND, APRIL 2002. HOMESICK AND LOVESICK. THE LOCUST, KÖLN, APRIL 2004. THE LOCUST ARE A BAND FROM SAN DIEGO. THEY WEAR LOCUST COSTUMES.

DINER, BALTIMORE, FEBRUARY 2002. BREAKFAST. **FERRY, FRANCE, APRIL 2002.** FROM FRANCE TO UK. **LUNCH WITH BRIAN AND MARK, LONDON, MARCH 2002.** MARK WAS THE HEAD OF YYY'S FIRST UK LABEL. ALSO, A GIANT CRAB ON THE WALL. **BRUNCH AT CRACKER BARREL, OHIO, MARCH 2002.** HIGHWAY COMFORT FOOD. CHEAP AND DELICIOUS.

TRAIN STATION, NAGOYA, OCTOBER 2003.
WITH THE LIARS IN JAPAN, WHERE MOST TRAVEL IS DONE BY BULLET TRAIN.

**HAT, AMSTERDAM, APRIL 2002.** KAREN LOST THIS HAT A FEW DAYS AFTER BUYING IT IN PARIS. SOMEHOW, IT TURNED UP A FEW YEARS LATER ON THE HEAD OF THE ROADIE FOR THE NORWEGIAN BAND GLUECIFER.

KAREN AND KEVIN AT THE TRAIN STATION, PARIS, APRIL 2002.
OUTSIDE A BROTHEL, HAMBURG, APRIL 2002. PROSTITUTION IS TOLERATED HERE.

KAREN, SHEFFIELD, APRIL 2002. HOMESICK AND LOVESICK. THE LOWEST PERIOD OF OUR FIRST UK TOUR.  ANGUS, TOKYO, OCTOBER 2003. ANGUS IS THE SINGER IN THE LIARS.  MAN, TOKYO, OCTOBER 2003. ASLEEP IN THE FOOD COURT ON THE EIGHTEENTH STORY OF A SHOPPING MALL.

4 AM IN HOTEL BED, KÖLN, AUGUST 2003. WOMAN ASLEEP.   4 AM IN HOTEL HALLWAY, LONDON, MARCH 2003. WINE AND CHEESE.
4 AM IN HOTEL LOBBY, OSLO, AUGUST 2003. CLARION HOTEL.

**BRIAN ON THE ROOF, LONDON, JUNE 2003.** BRIAN SPENDS AN HOUR BEFORE EVERY SHOW TUNING HIS DRUMS. **ON THE COVER, AUSTIN, MARCH 2002.** THE DAY AFTER SXSW. **ASIF, SAN FRANCISCO, SEPTEMBER 2003.** MANAGER FOR YYY. **OLD CITY, BOURGES, APRIL 2004.** LIVING POSTCARD #180.

BRIAN AFTER SHOW, MONTREAL, FEBRUARY 2004.  AARON, NYC, MARCH 2002.  AT MERCURY LOUNGE, BEFORE LIARS PLAYED.
BLOODY SNARE, KÖLN, APRIL 2004. GABE FROM THE LOCUST'S DRUM. HIS DRUMS ARE OFTEN COVERED IN BLOOD OR VOMIT AFTER A SHOW.

KAREN IN SPOTLIGHT, TOKYO, OCTOBER 2003.
BEFORE A TV-SHOW APPEARANCE.

CLOCKWISE FROM TOP LEFT: JSBX ONSTAGE, SACRAMENTO, SEPTEMBER 2002.   SOUNDCHECK, MANCHESTER, APRIL 2004.
BAR STOOLS, BOWLING GREEN, MARCH 2002.   JSBX, AMSTERDAM, APRIL 2002.   MONITOR TATTOOS, CHICAGO, NOVEMBER 2002.
KAREN BACKSTAGE, SAN FRANCISCO, SEPTEMBER 2003.

CLOCKWISE FROM TOP LEFT: HAR MAR ONSTAGE AND ON SOLANA, MINNEAPOLIS, NOVEMBER 2003. KAREN BEFORE THE CURTAIN ROSE, LAS VEGAS, OCTOBER 2002. DANCERS, SAN FRANCISCO, MARCH 2004. BRIAN WARMING UP, LOS ANGELES, SEPTEMBER 2003. STOLEN MASKS FROM THE BAND CLINIC, AUSTIN, MARCH 2002. BRIAN AND FACE GRAFFITI, SAN DIEGO, JUNE 2004.

GUY AND KAREN, DALLAS, NOVEMBER 2003. GUY IS A ONE-MAN BLUES BAND ALSO KNOWN AS ENTRANCE.
PLAYING DICE, LOS ANGELES, MARCH 2004. I WON $80 PLAYING "THREES."
HAR MAR SUPERSTAR, SYDNEY, OCTOBER 2003. AT THE LIVID FESTIVAL.

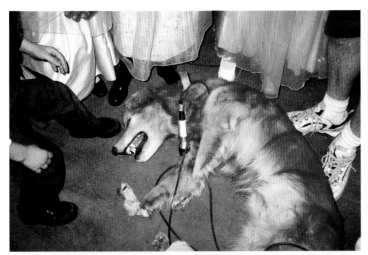

DEAD DOG, LOS ANGELES, JUNE 2004. GIRLS, LOS ANGELES, JUNE 2004. BOTH SHOT DURING THE MAKING OF THE YYY VIDEO FOR "Y-CONTROL."
HOTTER THAN HELL, KÖLN, AUGUST 2003. GERMANY HAS YET TO IMPLEMENT AIR-CONDITIONING IN ANY OF THEIR ROCK CLUBS, MAKING THE TEMPERATURES EASILY
REACH AROUND 120 DEGREES.

SOLANA, BERLIN, JUNE 2003. SOLANA OFTEN TOURS WITH YYY SELLING MERCH. **CONOR, ENGLAND, JUNE 2004.** ON THE BUS FROM GLASTONBURY FESTIVAL. **BRIAN, MONTREAL, AUGUST 2003.** NAPPING BEFORE OUR SHOW OPENING FOR BJÖRK.

BRIAN, OSAKA, OCTOBER 2003. AFTER YYY'S SECOND SHOW IN JAPAN.  SELF-PORTRAIT BAND PHOTO, PARIS, JUNE 2003. ON THE WAY TO SOUNDCHECK.
THE BIRD BLOBS, MELBOURNE, DECEMBER 2003. IN THE BACK OF A PIRATE COFFEE SHOP.

MYSTERY SURPRISE BAG, VERMONT, AUGUST 2003.  BACKSTAGE HOSPITALITY, SACRAMENTO, SEPTEMBER 2002.
DAVE WITH MERCHANDISE MONEY, LOS ANGELES, APRIL 2003.  HOUSE-PARTY REMNANTS, TUCSON, OCTOBER 2002.

BACKSTAGE HOSPITALITY, LONDON, JUNE 2003. DIVIDED BACKSTAGE HOSPITALITY, KÖLN, APRIL 2004. GIFT-SHOP SLAVERY ON HIGHWAY 90, MARCH 2002.
BACKSTAGE HOSPITALITY, DENVER, NOVEMEBER 2003. LATER COMPLETELY CONSUMED BY THE OPENING BAND.

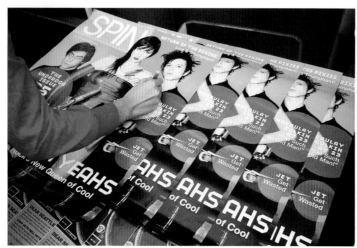

SIGNING SPIN POSTERS, LOS ANGELES, AUGUST 2004.   SEAT MARKERS, LOS ANGELES, JUNE 2004. AT THE MTV VIDEO MUSIC AWARD REHEARSALS.
SIGNING PROMO POSTERS, SAN FRANCISCO, MARCH 2004. POSTER PHOTO BY MICK ROCK.

SMASHED POSTER, BRISTOL, FEBRUARY 2003. YYY ALMOST BROKE UP THE NEXT DAY.  KAREN, ANTWERP, APRIL 2002. WITH A FRENCH MAGAZINE ABOUT THE SO-CALLED NEW YORK SCENE.  YYY POSTER, DUBLIN, APRIL 2002. THIS GUITAR, A GIFT,  WAS STOLEN THE NEXT YEAR IN BERLIN.  KICK DRUM, DENVER, NOVEMBER 2003. STENCIL BY KAREN.

YYY POSTERS, HAMBURG, AUGUST 2003. ALSO THE PHOTOGRAPHER'S BIRTHDATE. **GIANT NME POSTER, READING, UK, AUGUST 2003.** APPARENTLY, YOU PUT YOUR HEAD IN IT. **YYY POSTERS, BERLIN, JUNE 2003.** **CAKE, MASSACHUSETTS, NOVEMBER 2002.** YYY OPENED FOR SONIC YOUTH ON KAREN'S BIRTHDAY.

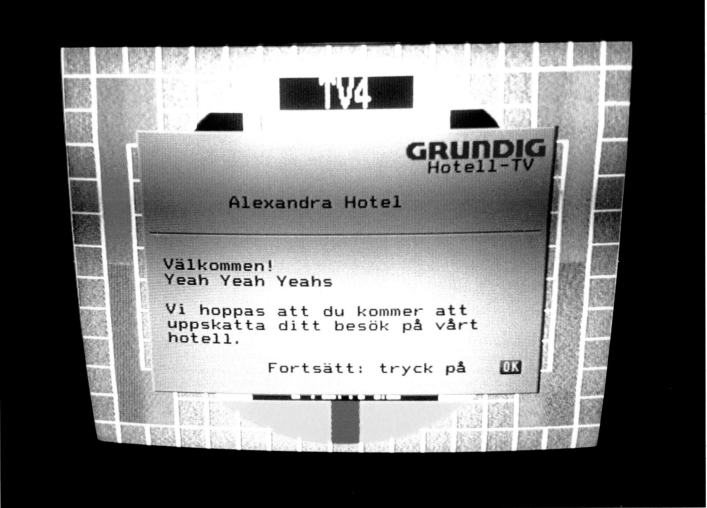

PHOTO-BOOTH PHOTOS, ORLANDO, NOVEMBER 2003.   MAGAZINES ON THE STREET, SYDNEY, OCTOBER 2003.   THIS IS WALLPAPER, LAS VEGAS, OCTOBER 2002.
HOTEL ROOM TV, STOCKHOLM, JULY 2002.

SOUNDCHECK IN MONTREAL, AUGUST 2003. OPENING FOR BJÖRK.  BLOW-UP DOLL, MELBOURNE, OCTOBER 2003. IT JUST APPEARED IN THE HALLWAY.
BJÖRK'S EQUIPMENT TRUCKS, MONTREAL, AUGUST 2003.  JON SPENCER, CANADIAN BORDER, SEPTEMBER 2002. ON TOUR WITH THE BLUES EXPLOSION, 5 A.M.

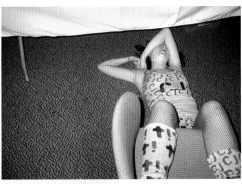 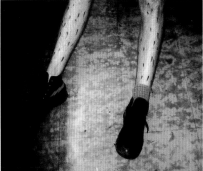 

KAREN, SEATTLE, SEPTEMBER 2003. IMMEDIATELY AFTER THE SHOW. **HAIRY LEGS, OSAKA, OCTOBER 2003. SSION DANCERS, CHICAGO, NOVEMBER 2003.** SSION ARE A BAND FROM KANSAS CITY. FOR THIS SHOW, THEY HAD DANCERS ON ROLLER SKATES. **WHITE STRIPES, LOS ANGELES, SEPTEMBER 2003.** SOUNDCHECK AT THE GREEK THEATRE.

# AN UNOBSTRUCTED VIEW

I remember a discussion I had with a girlfriend several years ago at a museum in Los Angeles. We were looking at a painting by Cy Twombly, and I remember feeling uneasy. "I don't get it" is what I was thinking, and "I feel stupid because I don't get it" is what I was feeling. But because I was in love with her and she was intelligent and ethereal and capable of thinking on a much deeper level about this sort of thing than I clearly could, I looked on in frustration.

Eventually she asked me what I thought. I started to flounder around with my answer, trying not to sound like a complete retard about why I didn't care for the painting. In a transparent attempt at saving face I switched gears and began talking about something I *did* like (a trick I learned in the Marines). Hoping this would allow me to walk out of there without my girlfriend thinking I was simple and dumping me for some quiet yet verbose, preciously sensitive art-history major with a thing for bouncy girls who hang out at museums (the best!).

So that's when I started to talk about photographs. I mentioned how they were probably my favorite purely visual medium. I had never really thought about why, but I found the reasons came very organically and without hesitation. Maybe because photography is ostensibly the least subjective art form. If you looked at Renoir's *Danseuse* (a painting of a young dancer you moron, learn French!) and said, "that looks like a painting of a young dancer and she looks like she's about to undergo a traumatic sexual experience with a family friend who lost an arm in an industrial accident and as a result has gangrene and you can tell the girl dancer is fucked up because her mom treats her like shit because she's secretly jealous of her youth and vitality and blah blah blah . . . " we could rightfully say to you, "What the fuck are you talking about, you pretentious asshole? That's not what Renoir intended. Have some more Nyquil and go back to sleep." BUT Nick's picture of messy hotel bed #53? Oh man! Can I imagine some stories about that! And now I'm onstage . . . in Stockholm! And wait! At this very instant I'm with this band after the show. I didn't know that an overhead shot of breakfast could stir up so many emotions and remind me of that time I was with Darcy and Todd and that girl from Barcelona at the Waffle House and T. J. locked himself in the women's restroom and called the radio station from his cell phone and then the cops came and . . .

I can look at a photo of, say, six people shot from behind, waiting on a train platform, and make up my own story about who they are, what's happening, what's about to happen and why. I can speculate as to the relationships they have with each other and their surroundings and what their status is to each other, and I will not be wrong even if I am. Maybe those people are in a band. Maybe they're not. I am God when I look at that photo, and my judgments are never too harsh or undeserved. It is whatever it is, was, and will be forever, fact *and* fiction! And this is what I like in particular about young Nick Zinner's photographs. They are evocative and lonely and inclusive and hopeful and specific and universal all at the same time.

— David Cross
Santa Barbara, 2005

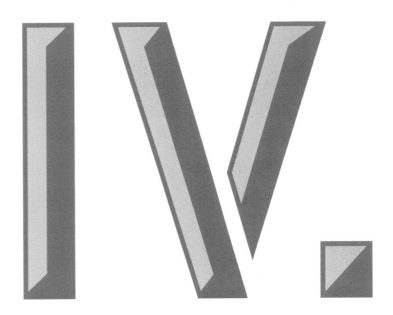

96

*Plane to London, May 2003*

*Plane to Japan, October 2003 / Plane from Japan, November 2003*

*Plane from Bali, October 2003*

*Plane to Bali, October 2003 / Birds, Brooklyn, October 2002*
*Jubilee Jets, London, June 2002 / Man on Flagpole, Berlin, July 2003*
*Plane from Sydney, October 2003 / Ocean, Byron Bay, December 2002*

Top: Hotel Lamp, Glasgow, February 2003 / Field, Kansas, November 2003 / Snowstorm, NYC, February 2003 / Trees, Tasmania, December 2002
Bottom: TV, Vancouver, September 2002 / Jackalope, North Dakota, April 2003 / Deer with Collar, Berlin, June 2003 / Schoolkids, London, June 2002

Sky, Portland, April 2003

Used Pantyhose, Detroit, October 2002 / Birthday Balloons, Brisbane, December 2002

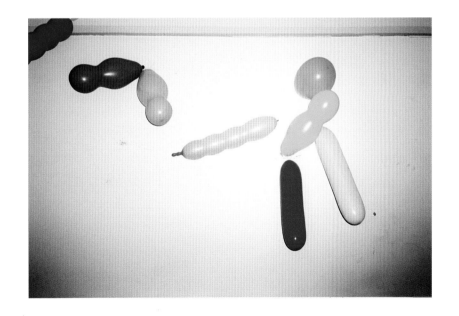

*Balloon Seller, Bali, October 2003 / Tents, Bordeaux, August 2003*
*UMA Flowers, Los Angeles, June 2004 / Pills, Brixton, April 2002*

*Park Flowers, Sydney, October 2003*

Dumpsters, Berlin, June 2003

Vomit, London, May 2003 / Cute Vacuum, London, August 2003

*Tokyo, October 2003 / Brisbane, October 2003*
*Detroit, October 2003 / Portugal, August 2003*
*Los Angeles, April 2003 / Brighton, April 2002*

*Tokyo, July 2004 / Berlin, July 2003*
*London, March 2003 / Köln, August 2003*
*London, January 2003 / Los Angeles, December 2002*

110

Père-Lachaise Cemetery, Paris, March 2003  /  Festival Sunset, Oslo, August 2003

*Postcard Setting, Porto, August 2003 / Overpass, Chicago, April 2003*

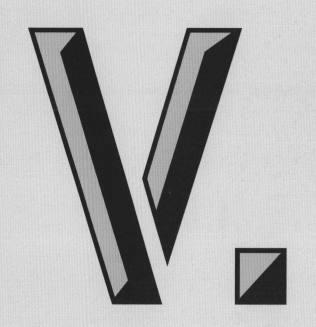

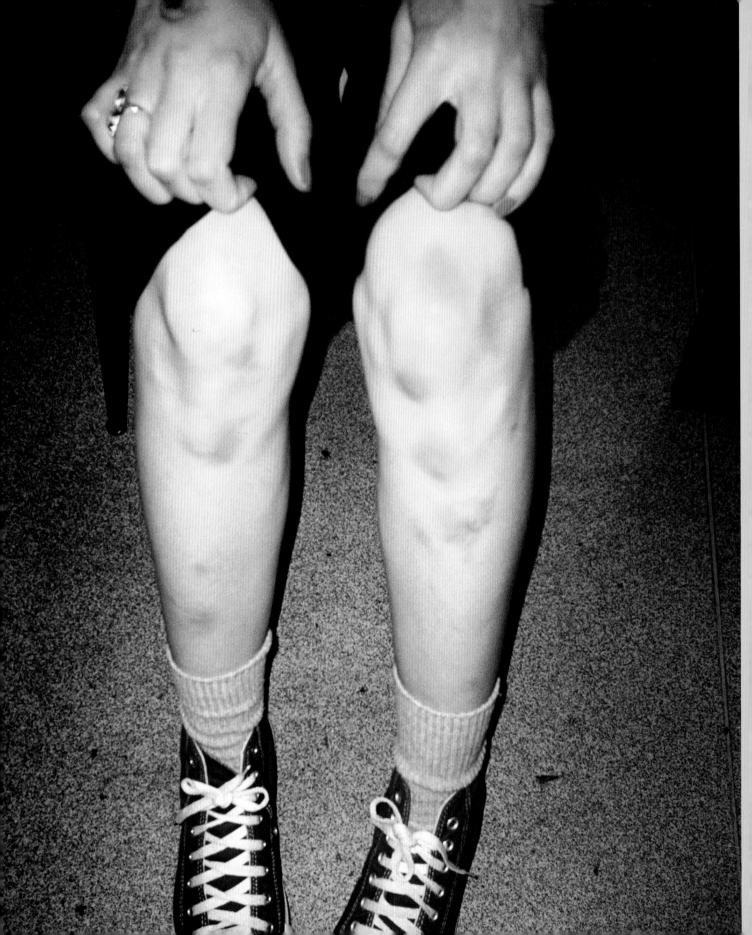

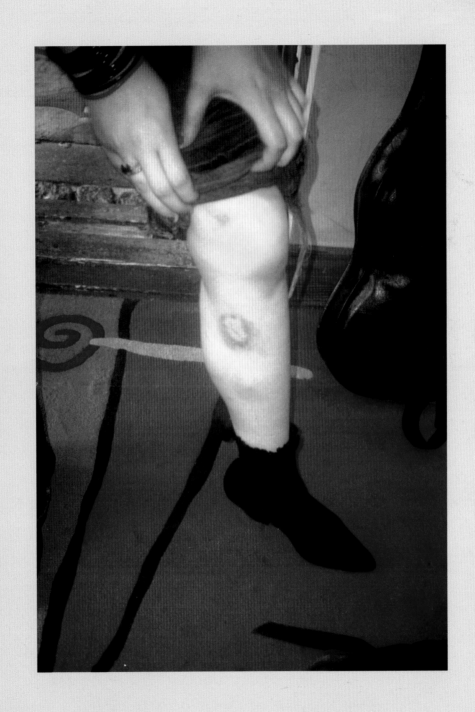

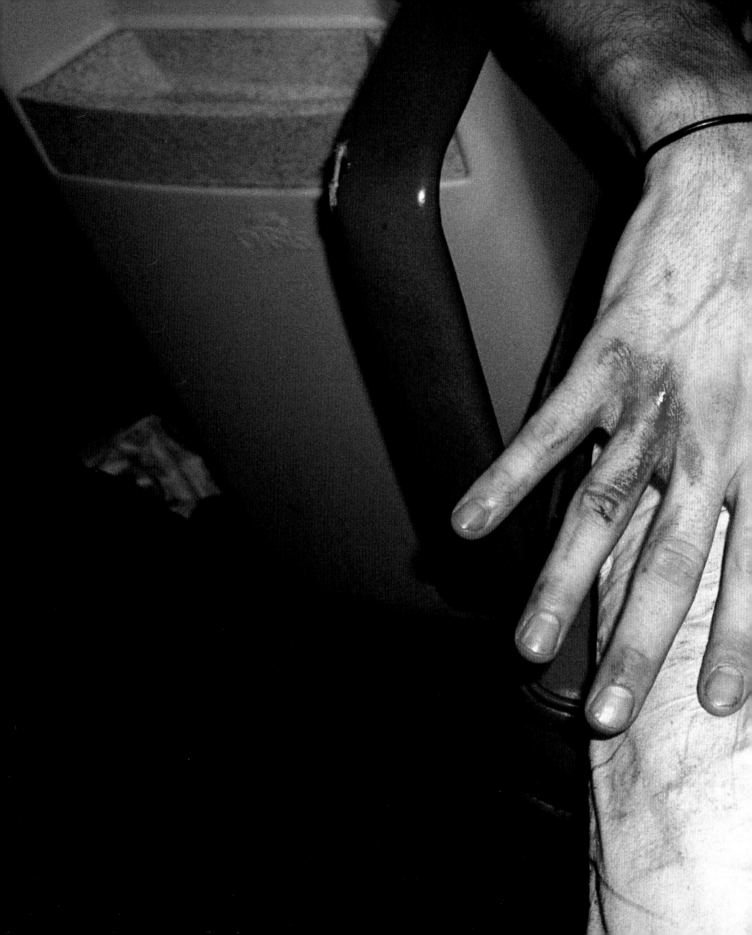

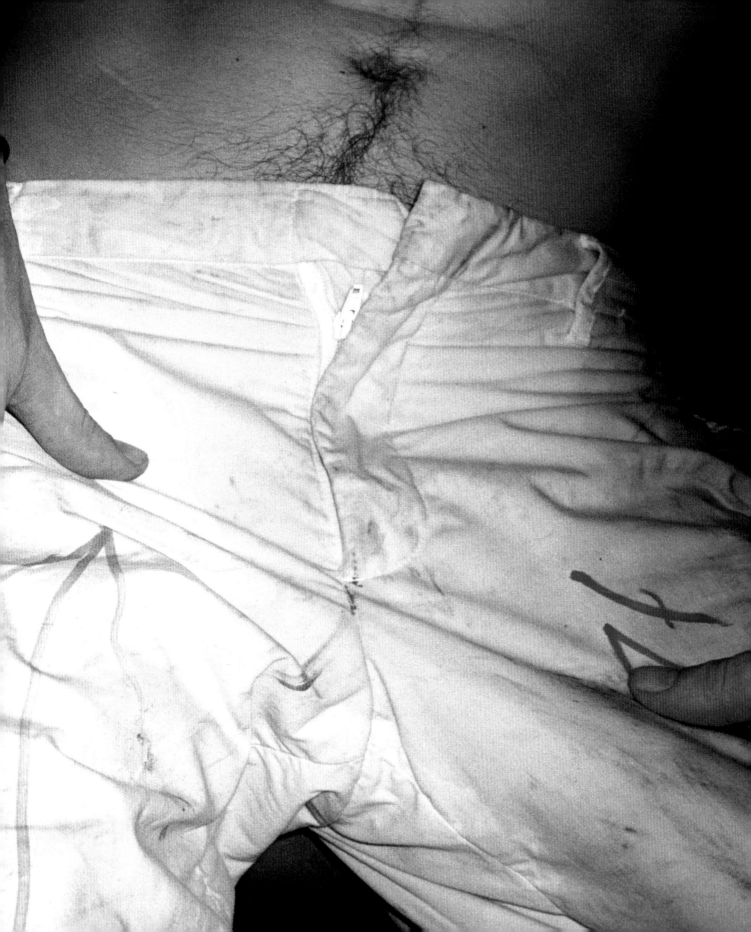

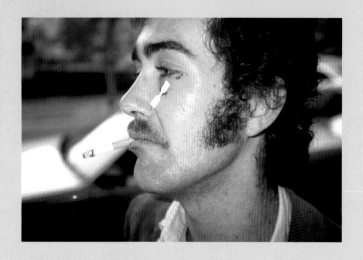

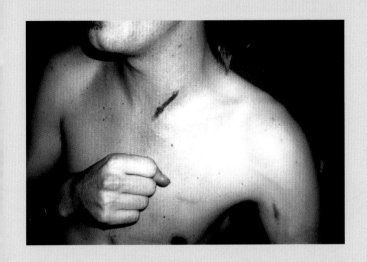

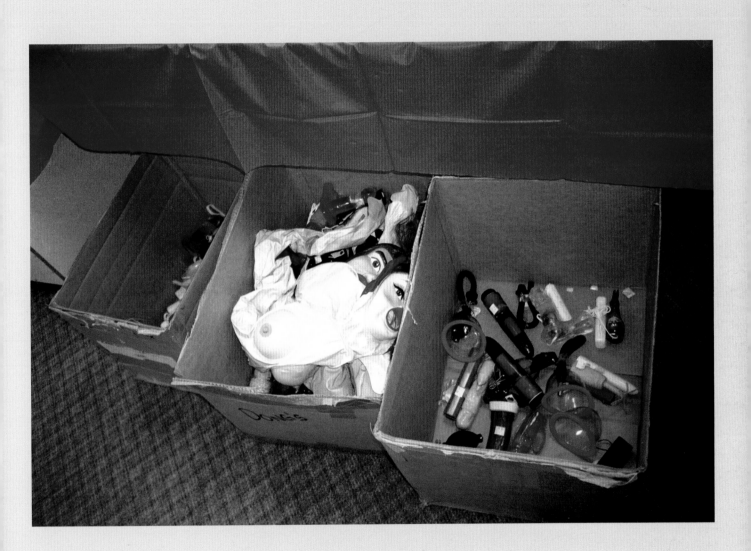

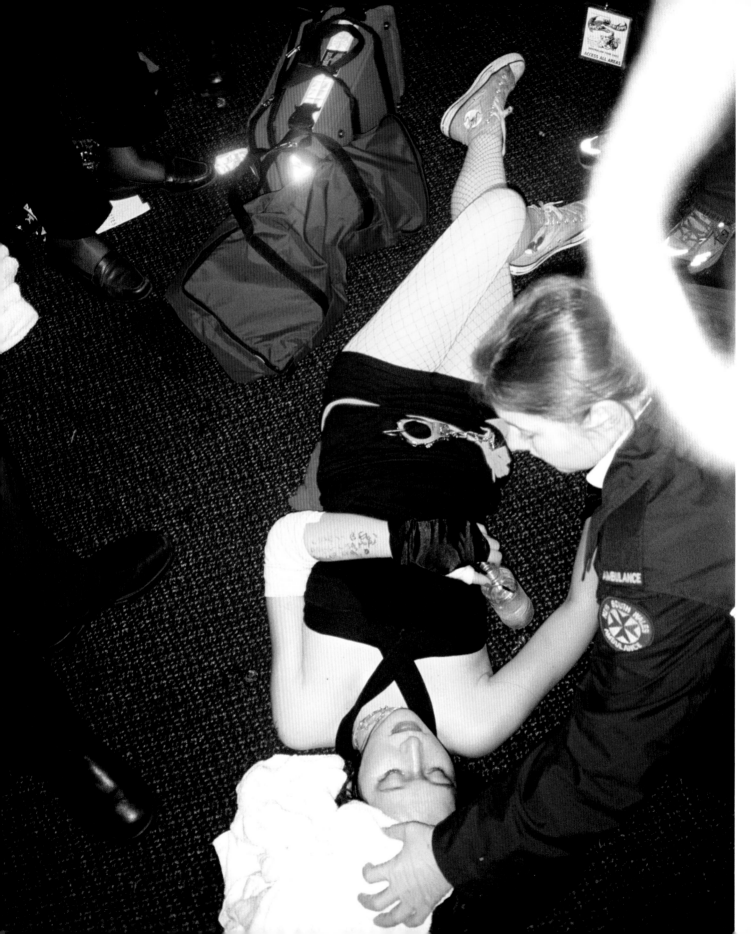

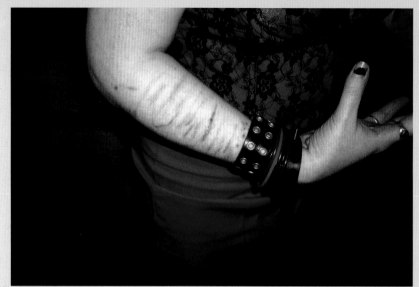

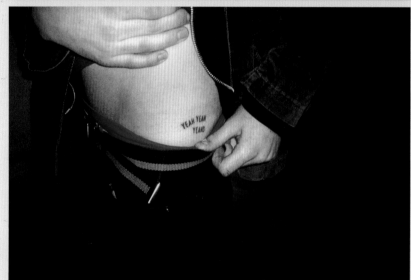

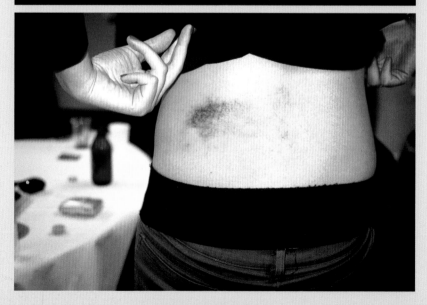

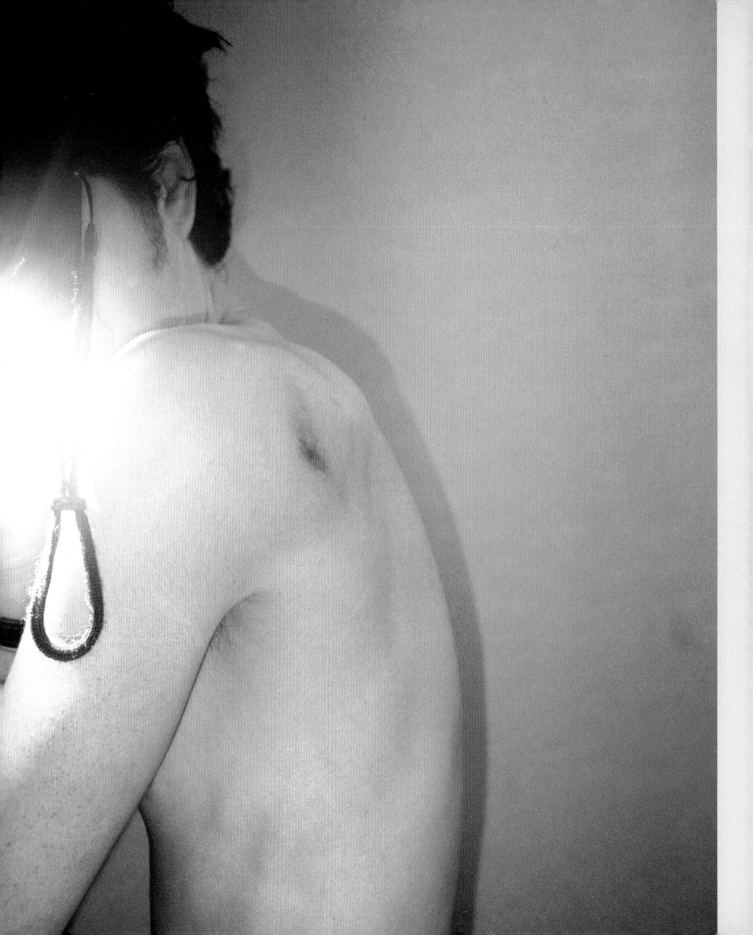

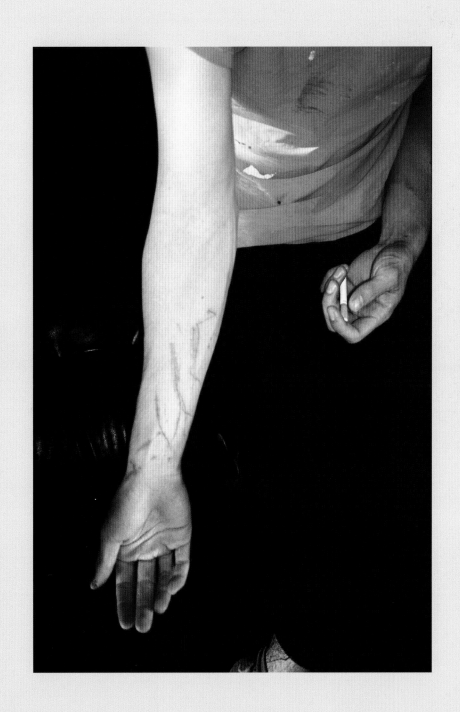

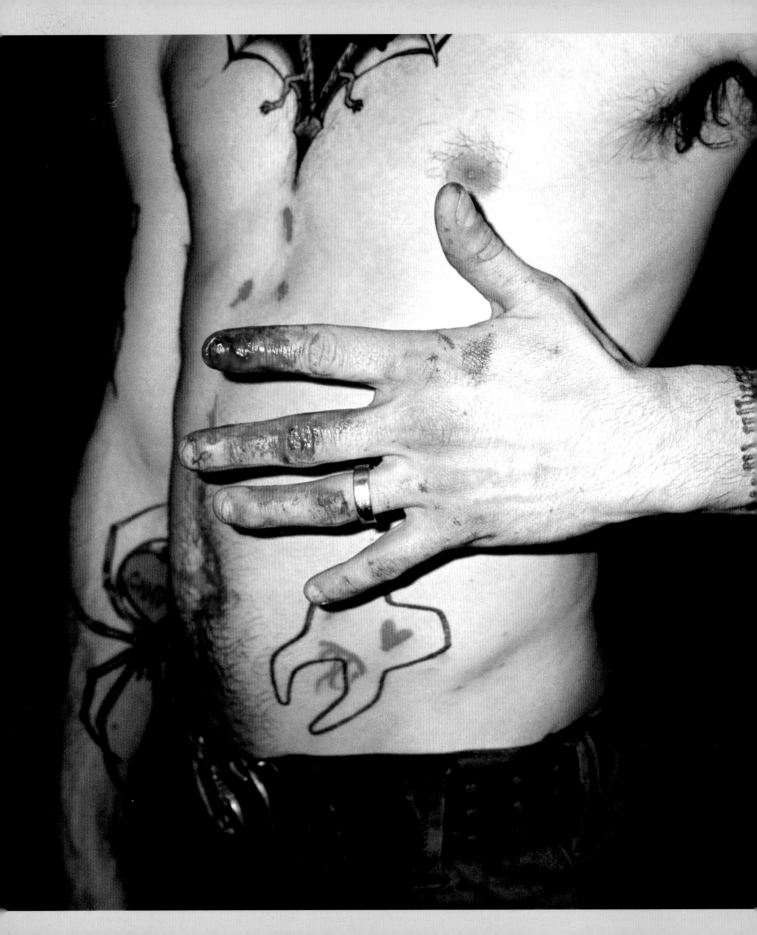

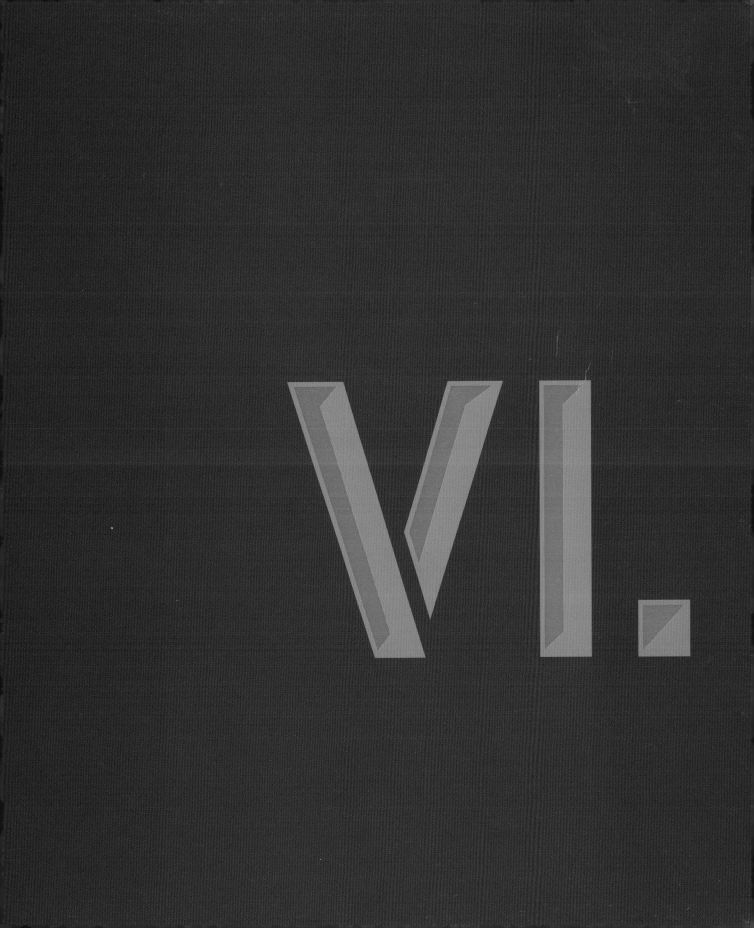

FRANCE AUGUST 2003

MELBOURNE OCTOBER 2003
SYDNEY OCTOBER 2003

SEATTLE  SEPTEMBER  2003
PORTUGAL  AUGUST  2003

CENTRAL PARK NEW YORK JULY 2004

146

PHILADELPHIA JULY 2004

147

NEW YORK  MAY 2003  /  POMONA  MARCH 2004
MONTREAL  FEBRUARY 2004  /  SYDNEY  OCTOBER 2003

MEXICO CITY  SEPTEMBER 2004  /  BRISTOL  MARCH 2003
GLASGOW  APRIL 2004  /  AUSTIN  NOVEMBER 2003

149

BRIGHTON APRIL 2004
DENVER NOVEMBER 2003

150

DALLAS   NOVEMBER 2003
AUSTIN   NOVEMBER 2003

151

LOS ANGELES  JUNE 2004

153

BROOKLYN AUGUST 2002
STOCKHOLM JULY 2002

155

POMONA  MARCH 2004

HAMBURG AUGUST 2003

157

TOKYO OCTOBER 2003

NEW YORK APRIL 2003

159

CHICAGO OCTOBER 2002 / SACRAMENTO SEPTEMBER 2002
NEW YORK MARCH 2003 / SAN FRANCISCO APRIL 2003

160

OXFORD MARCH 2003 / KÖLN APRIL 2004
CHICAGO OCTOBER 2002 / FUKUOKA OCTOBER 2003

161

CHICAGO OCTOBER 2002
CHICAGO APRIL 2003

FLORENCE   APRIL 2004
LOS ANGELES   MARCH 2004

CARDIFF APRIL 2002 / BOLOGNA APRIL 2004

165

OSLO AUGUST 2003

VII.

172

173

YOU
Call me Nick
077903039-
8
LUV
katy
Leila

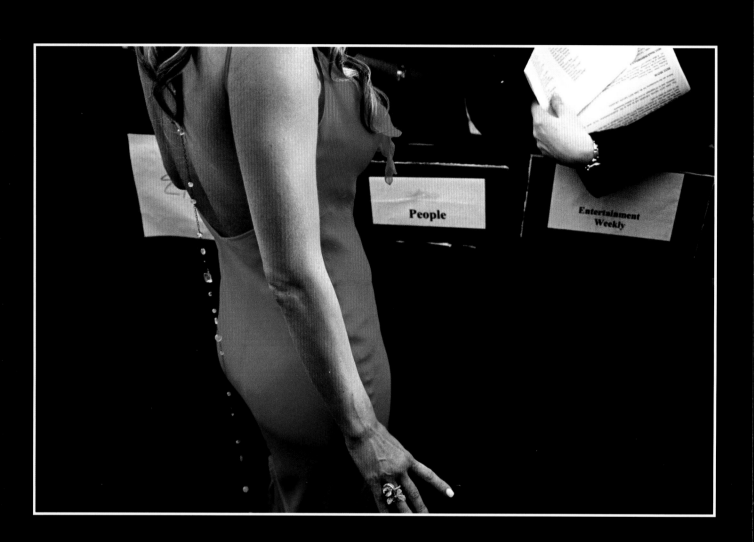

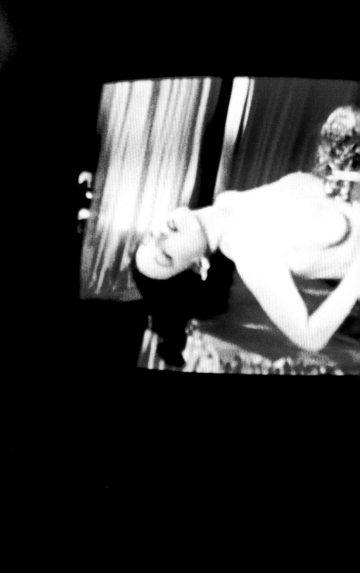

# VIII.

# NICK ZINNER
# IN CONVERSATION WITH
# JESSE PEARSON

JESSE: You started taking pictures in high school, right?

NICK: Yeah. My first girlfriend had a camera, and I used to take pictures of her in the forest, looking goth. I eventually took a photo class.

JESSE: Was it a regular public school?

NICK: I went to an alternative high school — a progressive liberal-arts place. So they actually nurtured the arts. My high school was like a breeding ground for future graduates or dropouts of colleges like Hampshire and Evergreen.

JESSE: So this girlfriend was inspirational because she had a camera in the first place.

NICK: Yeah, but then there was also a requirement at my school that you take a month off and do something productive with your life, for academic credit. So I went traveling around Europe with a friend of mine. That's when I started taking documentary-style photographs.

JESSE: Were you planning on taking a lot of pictures when you left on that trip?

NICK: Well, that's why I went, but it was way more unconscious than conscious. When you're in a new environment and you're kind of intimidated by it, the camera is the perfect tool to make sense of where you are and what you're seeing.

JESSE: And it's a nice way to distance yourself. You can sort of be there and not be there at the same time.

*Portland April 2003*
*Limerick April 2002*

NICK: That's actually what pushed me in the direction of taking pictures of people I knew and situations that I actually was in. After I had been doing travelogue stuff, I just got tired of that outsider perspective.

JESSE: Right, the foreign person in a foreign place.

NICK: In that situation, you're striving for something that you think is objective, but there's no way that it can be. So I went supersubjective and tried to focus on things that were happening around me that I would probably forget the next week [*laughs*].

JESSE: Was that shift to taking personal photos more about doing it for you, or was it about doing it to show other people what you  were enjoying in life or what your friends were like?

NICK: I never really think about the whole aspect of presenting photos to people. When I had that show at Gavin Brown's Enterprise last year or six months ago — whenever — when I put up five hundred photographs, I worked on it for three or four days straight, hanging it, but I didn't really make the connection that people I didn't know would actually be coming to see it and asking questions about it. I'm totally naïve in that way. So I went to the opening like an hour late.

DANCERS, BALI, 1995

JESSE: Were you nervous?

NICK: I was totally freaked out. I walked in and there were all these people like, "Hey, congratulations." And I was like, "What are you doing here?"

JESSE: "Why do you want to look at my fucking diary?"

NICK: Right! I had this really weird antagonistic reaction. It was totally fucked up. [*laughs*]

JESSE: Photographing is so different from making songs. I guess the ultimate goal is to get the song out to the world for sure.

NICK: Yeah. But even then it's not something you should really be conscious of while you're writing it. That kind of destroys everything.

JESSE: I'm interested in the fact that a photographer you really liked early on was Henri Cartier-Bresson.

NICK: I went to Bard College. They had a really good photo library there, and I also worked at a museum on the school grounds. I ended up spending all my free time looking at photo books. Cartier-Bresson was definitely the first one who really spoke to me.

JESSE: What about his work did you latch onto?

NICK: At the height of my documentary-photography period [*laughs*], I liked the fact that the whole approach was one person with a camera against the world. His thing was always the decisive moment, where random elements line up and present

Top:
Tasmania December 2002
Los Angeles December 2002

Middle:
Chicago March 2004
Paris April 2002

Bottom:
Oslo August 2003
Stockholm July 2002

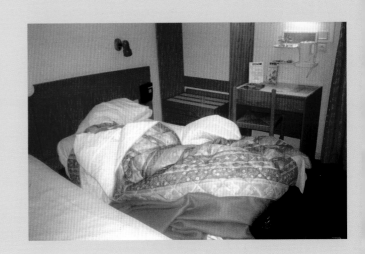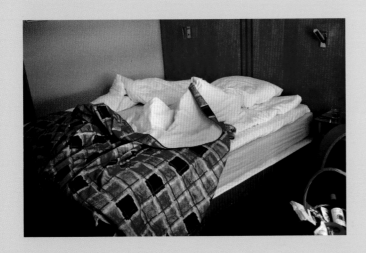

themselves in a very beautiful way. It was making something special out of nothing.

JESSE: His photos teach you how to look at things differently, to make observations you wouldn't have made otherwise.

NICK: Definitely. The things that I like most in his work are just gestures or a certain expression on somebody's face. Even though while it's happening it only lasts a second, it's something that is so powerful it can be frozen and declare a moment forever. It's basically the idea of a photo as a film still.

NUNS, PRAGUE, 1996

VATICAN, ROME, 1993

JESSE: But if you're too conscious of the decisive moment, you're not going to get it because you're going to photograph every moment, you know what I mean? You would be a stop-action *Sports Illustrated* photographer instead.

NICK: Exactly.

JESSE: So that makes me wonder if being a photographer makes you alter your behavior when you're out in the world. Do you try and put yourself in certain places because you're a photographer?

NICK: Sometimes. I don't really like to think of myself as a photographer, but I have put myself into really stupid situations much sooner than I should, just to see if I could get a good photo out of it.

JESSE: What kind of sketchy shit are we talking about?

NICK: I once got thrown out of a brothel in Indonesia.

JESSE: Jesus Christ.

NICK: Yeah, I know. That was kind of an example of like how far can I take it without actually getting hurt. I certainly wouldn't skulk about there looking for sex.

JESSE: Does that element of looking for some kind of dangerous or strange situation apply to photos of your friends, too? Is it about having the late night, being there when people are going to extremes?

NICK: I guess so, yeah. Extreme behavior is always the most interesting and the most fun [*laughs*]. The experience is usually more important than the photograph.

JESSE: Ok, so why the shift from travel and documentary pictures to personal things?

195

*Hamburg August 2003*
*San Francisco September 2003*

NICK: I showed some photos to a curator. He totally tore apart all my work.

JESSE: Did he call you an imperialist for going on vacation?

NICK: Yeah, a "visual colonialist."

JESSE: Oh man, is that a quote?

FLOOD, BALI, 1995

CEREMONY, BALI, 1995

NICK: Yeah [*laughs*].

JESSE: That's great. I'd love to get called a visual colonialist.

NICK: Even though I should have hit him, it was definitely an awakening. I realized that a photograph from someplace else was interesting because of the element of the unknown — exoticism. Edward Said talks about all this in his essay *Orientalism*. But that's such an empty aesthetic, because what's exotic to one person is totally normal to another. I have one photo that I took in Bali at a Hindu ceremony. It's just a photo of a bunch of people looking up, but in the background of these trees, there's like this floating spirit head. It looks just like Rama, the prince from the Ramayana story [*laughs*]. It's crazy. But I showed that to a Balinese kid I knew and I was like, "Wow, look at this insane photo!" He was like, "Uh, yeah. Yawn."

JESSE: It's like showing an American kid a picture of the Empire State Building. "Big whup."

NICK: Exactly, it's like nothing. I guess that was when I started to focus on things around me personally. I also got into this feeling of nostalgia.

JESSE: Nostalgia in what sense?

NICK: Maybe nostalgia for things that were happening in the present. Looking at things that were going on and knowing that half the people I was surrounded by I'd never see again, and they'd probably die before me. Or vice-versa.

JESSE: That's interesting because — and I never know how to say things like this gracefully — but that's so all about this fucking subculture or culture that we're both involved in where almost every night you meet people you might not ever see again. Usually around dawn.

NICK: Yeah.

*Nagoya October 2003*
*Portland April 2003*

JESSE: And you do things that are a little more nutty. It's not like frat brothers, where they'll know each other for eighty years. I've forgotten more people in New York than I've known intimately anywhere else. So you started to become aware of that too?

NICK: Yeah, and embrace it.

JESSE: Do you have a lot of pictures of people you don't even remember anymore?

CLUB GIRLS, NEW YORK, 1999

NICK: Most of my pictures are like that [*laughs*]. These are chance encounters. Even the crowd photos at Yeah Yeah Yeahs shows feel that way to me.

JESSE: That makes sense.

NICK: All those crowd pictures are about places and events that could only have happened at that time with that collection of people.

JESSE: It's almost like the concept of occasional poetry, where you write a poem only to memorialize a certain occasion, like a wedding or a wake.

NICK: That's true.

JESSE: Did you move to Brooklyn after college?

NICK: Yeah, into an apartment with a friend of mine I was playing in a band with. There are about two years of photographs from that time, which are only of my friends. Or of friends in bands. It seemed to me that going to New York and doing street photography or whatever would have been the most boring thing, like why should I do that?

JESSE: You have to get in line to take a picture of a choice piece of urban decay in New York anyway.

NICK: Totally, it's like four photographers for every homeless person [*laughs*].

JESSE: You worked in a darkroom for a while, right? What did that experience teach you about photography?

NICK: I worked in several black-and-white labs. It was probably the least constructive thing I could possibly have done, but I was broke, and it was the only skill I had besides delivering pizzas. I worked with good people and had free darkroom access, but there's nothing like spending ten hours a day printing wedding and fashion pictures to make you completely disinterested in being creative. I got so bored with the medium. That's a reason why I bought a point-and-shoot camera, switched to color, and started dropping my film off at crappy Chinatown photomats.

*Paris June 2004*
*Beverly Hills May 2004*

JESSE: Do you still prefer shooting in color?

NICK: If I had more time to print now, I'd shoot more black and white. It abstracts everything in a really beautiful way. It's almost too easy, like putting reverb all over your record. It will sound good no matter what.

COUPLE, BROOKLYN, 1999

JESSE: Ha, that's true.

NICK: A producer friend of mine told me that Depeche Mode used to say: "Reverb = girls." They said that if you put reverb on your songs, more people will buy your records, more people will go to your shows, and more girls will come backstage or whatever. Anyway, color is much less sentimental. Color is unforgiving.

JESSE: Was there ever a time when you felt discouraged as a photographer?

NICK: When I first moved to New York, I went around to some galleries and magazines and showed my portfolio. Everyone was like, "You have too many styles, it's confusing to look at," and I sort of went, "Err, fuck you," and stopped showing things to people. I gave up all aspirations of being a "professional photographer" or whatever, and just did things for myself. It was kind of a relief, because in New York everyone is a fucking photographer. You go to a protest or the Halloween parade and you can't even see anything because all these dudes with Leicas and tan vests are all up in your shit.

JESSE: How did your social life change when you first moved to the city? I know that when I got out of college and came here it was like this explosion of going out every night, a totally different mode of hanging out.

NICK: Oh yeah. You go out and meet people and sleep with people and do bad things every single night.

JESSE: Then you burn out after a year and spend three months as a hermit.

NICK: Exactly.

JESSE: Then you get back in it.

NICK: Or you drop in for visits, and sometimes they're extended visits.

JESSE: Do you think the people you were hanging out with then thought of you as a photographer? Did you have your camera out a lot?

Copenhagen August 2003
Los Angeles October 2003

NICK: Not that much. I think for awhile I got tired of having it around. I let my camera sleep.

JESSE: Was it because you weren't finding pictures you liked, or were you feeling self-conscious about it?

NICK: I was unsure of what I was doing. The classic postgraduate conundrum. I knew I still had this instinct to react to things photographically. I probably started taking pictures more and more again whenever I was leaving a circle of friends. I also got a point-and-shoot camera then, which made it much more of a socially possible extension.

JESSE: Point-and-shoots increase the immediacy of picture taking so much, but they also look really casual, like something your grandma could use. Did you ever find people were performing for you when the camera came out?

NICK: Maybe for the first five minutes it was out, but after that, no. I guess it's different now that everyone on the planet has a Yashica T4 camera, but five or six years ago it seemed the only people who were really conscious of getting their picture taken were other photographers.

JESSE: Now it's everybody, every high school kid. Did you start getting into contemporary photographers at any point? Did you ever have a period where you found someone like Nan Goldin inspirational?

NICK: When I first saw her work I thought it was really kind of crap. I was like, she's just taking pictures of her friends [*laughs*]. Then I realized that was a good thing. They're actually beautiful documents as well. It seemed like she also had — not that I'm comparing myself to her — but she also had that sense of like a dying time in her photos.

JESSE: That's an interesting thing, though, because to be inspired by that and for that to continue to work you kind of need to perpetually feel like you're in a dying time, right?

NICK: Yeah.

JESSE: Do you still feel that way?

NICK: Things move so fast in New York, and bands don't last forever so yeah, absolutely.

JESSE: Very Buddhist — just kidding. I want to touch a little bit on how your photography was affected by your band getting bigger and moving out into the world more. Were you overwhelmed by it at first?

NICK: When things started to get busy with us and we started to get a lot of attention, we all knew that it was almost a fluke.

*Boston September 2003*
*Sydney December 2003*

JESSE: That's a funny way of looking at it.

NICK: I'd already played in a rock band for a couple of years, and I'd never seen any band from New York get signed. Suddenly we were getting courted by record labels every night, and soon after that other New York bands were too.

JESSE: That moment must have been strange for you guys.

KAREN AT THE COOLER, FEBRUARY 2001

NICK: Yeah. It wasn't the reason that Yeah Yeah Yeahs started, so we all took this detached view on it. And also it was such an insane experience that I knew that taking photos of what was happening then and looking back on it a year or two or ten from that time would probably be the only way I would understand it.

JESSE: What was that period like?

NICK: I started getting freaked out really early on. I mean, we had songs in the top five of a dozen college radio stations when we were still making and assembling CDs in my apartment, way before any labels were involved. Trying to get good shows in other cities was impossible, but nightclubs in Sweden somehow were playing our music and kids were freaking out to it. The first realization that things were getting really crazy was probably when we played at South by Southwest in Austin in 2002. We were touring in a minivan, and Dave Sitek, now of TV On The Radio, was with us to help drive and roadie. We were supposed to play at a tiny club as part of the Kill Rock Stars showcase. But a day or two before we got there we found out that we'd been moved to a much larger room, like a thousand-person-capacity place, because SxSW was worried that the demand to see us would be so large it would be a fire hazard in a smaller club. We played first, and the room was packed with A&R people and curiosity seekers from all over the world. When we finished, the room cleared out and stayed half-empty the rest of the night.

JESSE: So that's a pretty clear sign that you were the most exciting thing there that year.

NICK: The next morning we were on the front page of both newspapers about the festival. We were all like, "Fuck!"

JESSE: Oh, and that's the other thing about getting bigger. Not just bigger venues, but you're dealing with the press. Which is a pretty mixed bag, to say the least.

NICK: Totally. During our first European and UK tour, we did so much press, like eight interviews every day, all with pretty much

the same questions. "Where are you guys from, why no bass player, what's this New York scene really like?" Brian and I were flying home from London and the stewardess was handing out landing cards. She came up to us and asked, "Where are you from?" We both spat out, "Brooklyn!"

JESSE: That's hilarious, but it also probably reflects the heavy burnout you must have been feeling.

NICK: I had some breakdowns, and so did Karen. We didn't feel like we deserved all the attention we were getting. When the band started, we were bored and angst ridden and never thought anything would come of it. So there were several times where we almost broke up out of confusion and fighting and pressure. But it happens to a lot of bands, you know? They lose sight of the reasons they first started and begin to care more about the band than about the people in the band and what they're creating. Then it's over.

JESSE: So maybe even all through that time, the camera was a distancing measure to maintain some sanity.

NICK: Yeah.

JESSE: Because when you put the camera between your face and what's happening, you're kind of mediating the reality of it, right?

NICK: Totally. And every day was kind of more intense than the last one, so I needed that.

207

JESSE: Do you build up a big stock of film and then get it all processed at once?

NICK: Usually I do it in batches. Every time we come back from a tour I'll have thirty or forty rolls of film. I just get drugstore prints. It's good because it's the only way to make sense of what just happened, of what tour happened. It sounds kind of stupid — maybe Henry Rollins is the person to talk about this [*laughs*] — but being on tour is a fantasy world.

JESSE: Of course. That doesn't sound stupid.

NICK: Nothing about it is normal, and if you're playing mostly the same songs every night to different people at different places, it's really easy to make them blend together. Karen especially, after every tour she collapses for two or three weeks.

JESSE: Yeah, she must be fucking drained.

NICK: Completely mentally and physically exhausted.

*Boston June 2003*
*Glasgow April 2004*

JESSE: I'm remembering different things I've read about touring and conversations I've had with people who've done it. It's a common thing on tour to detach from your body. Like, get up, play a show, go out, get up, play a show, go out, get up play a show . . .

So once again, the camera is like an anchor. How much of a chance do you get when you're on tour to take pictures in the towns that you're visiting?

NICK: On the earlier tours there wasn't really any time. We were in vans and always either driving or sleeping, so pretty much all I would see would be highways, venues, and hotels. It was like, "Oh look! We're in Milan!" But we would have to drive for six hours after the show. Then we started touring in a bus, which made things much better. You sleep on the bus and wake up in the city that you're going to play at in the afternoon, and usually have three or four hours to walk around before sound check or press or dinner. Also, if we play somewhere far away like Japan or Australia, at the end of the tour I'll try and stay for a week or two. Just to hang out, take pictures and run around.

JESSE: I'm wondering what it's like to photograph one person over a lot of time, the way you've done with Karen, and Brian as well.

NICK: Yeah, on tour, I take pictures of them at least three or four times a day.

JESSE: Do you think that they have some aspect of performance going when you take out the camera?

NICK: No. They have none. Everyone we've traveled with or toured with, after the first day or two, just continues what they're doing if the camera comes out. Although I do have a lot of stupid face photos.

JESSE: I'd hate to have images of people looking to the side — like that fucking emo photograph thing, that look-to-the-side face that everybody does.

NICK: Like a Myspace or Friendster photo.

JESSE: Exactly.

JESSE: What's the editing process of this book been like? How much stuff did you start with?

NICK: I started with something like nine or ten thousand photos.

JESSE: Are you serious? From how many years?

NICK: Like four and a half years. Every time I get film back, I put the ones I like aside. Six or seven months ago, I started going through everything again — every negative — and that was almost like starting fresh because there were all these things that at the time I didn't think were interesting that I like now.

JESSE: Was that about time passing, or was it more thinking about the pictures in terms of a book?

NICK: Both, definitely. It's kind of amazing how much people age

*Berlin June 2003*
*Orlando November 2003*

even in four years. I also wanted to edit out pictures that might seem exploitative of my friends. I didn't want to put in too many photos with sex and drugs because it's such a cliché for a musician.

JESSE: Is there one picture or kind of picture of yours that, when you think, "I'm a photographer," pops into your head? I guess I want you to say that you feel that way about the crowd shots [*laughs*]!

BRIAN, DURHAM, 2002

KAREN AT THE BLACK CAT, DC, MARCH 2002

NICK: It'd probably be the crowd shots. Usually I'll do three or four at each show. It used to be only one, but as the venues and stages and crowds have gotten bigger, I have to do more. It's interesting to do a few because on the first shot, people haven't noticed that I'm taking their picture. So on that one there are just people in the middle of a rock-show moment, maybe just staring straight ahead or caught up in that experience — or sometimes looking totally bored, like, this band sucks. And then as the people get aware of the camera, they start freaking the fuck out [laughs].

JESSE: Do you go out and meet your fans and take pictures of them face-to-face? What's that like?

NICK: It's good usually, but I guess it depends on where it is. I always try to go out and watch the other bands that we're playing with. Sometimes I can talk to people and just get other people's stories, which is rad. But sometimes, like in England, where the whole celebrity culture is so sensational, it can be hard to go out. I'll get hounded for autographs, and people'll be taking pictures on their cell phones. That's weird — people aren't supposed to interact like that. Sometimes it's fun, too, but it's a totally different experience, and it can be very distracting.

JESSE: I blame the British music press for that. Every band that comes out is the second coming of Christ. It's scary.

NICK: Totally. They build you up so they can throw you down.

JESSE: The slept-in-beds photos are such a perfectly realized series. Did those develop when you realized you'd been randomly taking photos of beds, or did you set out to document an aspect of touring and go: "These things I sleep in every night are interesting"?

NICK: It developed over time. I like to sleep a lot, and I used to do this project when I first moved to New York where I would photograph myself sleeping with one exposure, like a seven- or nine-hour exposure. I also liked this series that Uta Barth did where she would have people pose against a wall or whatever, then when they moved out of the frame, she would take the photo, trying to capture the person's essence. Beds always felt that way to me, like they held remnants of sleep and dreams but in and of themselves were very lonely. Anyway, at this point, I feel guilty if I don't take a picture of a bed I've slept in.

JESSE: You know, there was also a series Sophie Calle did where she had people come sleep in her bed and photographed them. Are there any other series-oriented works that inspired you? And in Terry Richardson's early book *Son of Bob*, there's a whole series where he would photograph a meal on the plate before he ate it, and then as a pile of shit in his toilet a while later.

NICK: Oh weird. I know a bunch of people who've done that. I also like the Bechers' work, where they travel around and photograph outdated factory and farm machinery from the exact same perspective, then show them in giant grids. It's very German. I like old high school yearbook photos, too, as long as they're not of me.

OVERNIGHT SLEEPING EXPOSURE, 1998

JESSE: What's your favorite kind of bed?

NICK: I'm quite happy if there are two fat pillows, a nice firm mattress with jersey beech cotton sheets, and no bedbugs, wet dogs, or dirty hippies in sight [*laughs*].

JESSE: So what are you going to do in the next couple months? You're multitasking so much. If I were you, I'd want to hide in a cave for a year.

NICK: I try not to think too much about what I'm doing or what I'm going to photograph. Overanalysis breeds mediocrity. I'm doing a bunch of new music projects with people whose work I admire. And, maybe do some short films about some of my friends who make music — just without any journalistic pretensions! As soon as I'm done scanning all the photos for this book, I'm going to Japan for a month to write music and clear my head.

*New York City, February 2005*

Chicago April 2003

Seattle March 2004

Orlando November 2003

Austin November 2003

Malmö July 2002

Porto August 2003

Tokyo January 2005

Tucson October 2002

London June 2002

Brixton April 2002

Bourges April 2004

Los Angeles September 2004

Göteborg July 2002

San Francisco September 2003

London April 2004

Melbourne October 2003

Bali October 2003

Limserick April 2002

Tucson October 2002

Boston June 2003

London June 2003

Chicago November 2003

Paris June 2003

Portland April 2003

Colby, Kansas November 2003

Tokyo October 2003

San Francisco April 2003

London August 2003

Sydney December 2002

Omaha November 2003

# CONTRIBUTORS

Nicholas Zinner plays guitar in the band Yeah Yeah Yeahs and other collaborative projects such as Bright Eyes and Head Wound City. He studied photography at Bard College and has published work in magazines such as *Vice*, *Black Book*, and *Rolling Stone*. Nick lives mostly in New York City.

Designer Stacy Wakefield lives in upstate New York. She and her sister, Amber Gayle, have published artists' books and zines under the imprint Evil Twin Publications since 1995. Stacy studied design at Amsterdam's Rietveld Academie and has worked as design director at *index* and *Artforum* magazines.

Born in Akron, Ohio, Jim Jarmusch lives and works in New York. His feature films include *Permanent Vacation* [1980], *Stranger Than Paradise* [1984], *Down By Law* [1986], *Mystery Train* [1989], *Night on Earth* [1991], *Dead Man* [1995], *Year of the Horse* [1997], *Ghost Dog: The Way of the Samurai* [1999], and *Coffee and Cigarettes* [2004].

Zachary Lipez lives in New York City where he tends bar and performs in the band Freshkills. He has published two books of poetry with Evil Twin Publications, *No Seats on the Party Car* [2001] and *Slept in Beds* [2003].

David Cross runs Whispers, an art gallery in Santa Barbara dealing mainly in watercolors. He has written several children's books under the nom de plume Hermoine Tifflebee. He can also be seen on Channel 5's *Doodles and Baubles* with Dr. James Greyson.

Jesse Pearson edits *Vice* magazine in New York City. His zine, *Catholic*, cofounded and edited with Glynnis McDaris, is published yearly by Evil Twin and D.A.P. Jesse's writing has appeared in *Sound Collector*, *Big*, *Parkett*, and *index*.